365 Things
Every Tea Lover
Should Know

HARVEST HOUSE PUBLISHERS

EUGENE, OREGON

Cover by Garborg Design Works, Savage, Minnesota

365 THINGS EVERY TEA LOVER SHOULD KNOW
Copyright © 2008
Published by Harvest House Publishers
Eugene, Oregon 97402
www.harvesthousepublishers.com

ISBN-13: 978-0-7369-2250-0

Printed in the United States of America

11 12 13 14 / BP-SK / 10 9 8 7 6 5 4 3 2

TAKING TIME FOR TEA

Tea. Such a small word, yet it evokes a universe overflowing with ideas, traditions, flavors, history, utensils, exotic travels, inventions, recipes, industry, and social graces. It's a near-endless list of fascinating details and pleasures.

Whether you are new to tea or have long sipped from its cup of inspiration, you will find among these pages many reasons to celebrate the beverage that symbolizes warmth, comfort, and generosity throughout the world.

The freshly poured cup equally nurtures conversation and silence. Community and solitude. Rejoicing and reflection. Giving and receiving. This is the abundance and wonder of tea! Take a sip and savor all it has to offer.

1

When making a great pot of tea, pour hot water into the teapot to warm it while the kettle of water is heating.

2

My dear, if you could give me a cup of tea to clear my muddle of a head I should better understand your affairs.

CHARLES DICKENS

3

Iced tea was invented at the 1904 St. Louis World's Fair by an expatriate Englishman named Richard Blechynden. His hot tea wasn't selling so he poured it over ice and had an instant success.

4 *The path to heaven passes through a teapot.*

ANCIENT PROVERB

5 In early eighteenth century Britain, tea was served in coffeehouses, which were restricted to men only. If women wanted tea from these locations, they had to have a man purchase the tea for them.

6 Keemun is from China and is known as the "burgundy of teas." It is full-bodied with a light taste.

7 There are four major tea types—black, oolong, green, and white.

8

Black tea undergoes the longest process of oxidation.

9

White tea undergoes the least amount of processing.

10

I smile, of course,
And go on drinking tea.
"Yet with these April sunsets, that somehow recall
My buried life, and Paris in the Spring,
I feel immeasurably at peace, and find the world
To be wonderful and youthful, after all."

T.S. ELIOT

11

When creating a great pot of tea, fill the teakettle with fresh, cold water. Then put the kettle on to boil.

12

Social life in the first half of the eighteenth century became more sophisticated as the coffeehouse gave way to the tea garden, a social melting pot where royalty and the masses could promenade together.

13

Silver jasmine is a delicate flower that adds a sweet fragrance and light flavor to green tea.

14

Teatime is by its very nature a combination of small luxuries arranged in social symmetry. And although tea for one is certainly a fine thing, the addition of a circle of dear friends to share it with ensures the whole is larger than its parts.

AUTHOR UNKNOWN

15

All you're supposed to do is every once in a while give the boys a little tea and sympathy.

ROBERT ANDERSON

16

As the centerpiece of a cherished ritual, it's a talisman against the chill of winter, a respite from the ho-hum routine of the day.

SARAH ENGLER

17

He brewed his tea in a blue china pot, poured it into a chipped white cup with forget-me-nots on the handle, and dropped in a dollop of honey and cream. He sat by the window, cup in hand, watching the first snow fall. "I am," he sighed deeply, "contented as a clam. I am a most happy man."

ETHEL POCHOCKI, *WILDFLOWER TEA*

18

Russian Caravan is a mellow black tea with the smoky flavor of Lapsang Souchong. It is an ideal tea to drink throughout the day.

19 BLACK CURRANT ICED TEA

6 black currant tea bags

2 cups boiling water

¼ cup sugar

3 cups cold water

cranberry juice

ice

—————————

Pour boiling water over tea bags.

Steep 90 seconds; then remove bags.

Stir in sugar and cold water.

Add a splash of cranberry juice and ice.

SANDY LYNAM CLOUGH,
THE ART OF TEA AND FRIENDSHIP

20

*For if I could please myself I would always
live as I lived there. I would choose always to
breakfast at exactly eight and to be at my desk
by nine, there to read or write till one. If a cup
of good tea or coffee could be brought to me
about eleven, so much the better. Tea should be
taken in solitude.*

C.S. LEWIS, *SURPRISED BY JOY*

21

The legend of tea's origin is that it
was discovered by Chinese Emperor
Shen Nung in 2737 BC, when a tea
leaf accidentally fell into a bowl of
hot water.

22

Lemon Balm is a lemony herbal tea also
known as "gentle balm" or "sweet balm."

23

Teapot is on, the cups are waiting,
Favorite chairs anticipating,
No matter what I have to do,
My friend, there's always time for you.

AUTHOR UNKNOWN

24

New to tea or have friends who are?
Plan a fresh kind of tea party...a tea-
tasting party. Arrange to serve black,
green, and oolong teas along with a
variety of extra flavor enhancers.

25

Why, the club was just the quietest place in the
world, a place where a woman could run in to
brush her hair and wash her hands, and change
her library book, and have a cup of tea.

KATHLEEN THOMPSON NORRIS,
SATURDAY'S CHILD

26

Rooibos (pronouncedd roy-boos) grows
in South Africa, and its needle-like leaves
are fermented like tea.

27

If you live in Canada, you might be
savoring Red Rose tea. This brand
was created in 1899 out of a blend
of Indian and Sri Lankan teas rather
than the more common Chinese and
Japanese teas. The result was a big
success in Canada and Britain.

28

And I who always keep the golden mean,
Have just declined my seventh cup of green.

HARTLEY COLERIDGE

29

Now stir the fire, and close the shutters fast,
Let fall the curtains, wheel the sofa round,
And, while the bubbling and loud hissing urn
Throws up a steamy column and the cups
That cheer but not inebriate, wait on each,
So let us welcome peaceful ev'ning in.

WILLIAM COWPER

30

I believe it is customary in good society to
take some slight refreshment at five o'clock.

OSCAR WILDE

31

Strange how a teapot can represent at the same
time the comforts of solitude and the pleasures
of company.

AUTHOR UNKNOWN

32
Tea absorbs moisture. Be sure to store
loose tea or tea bags in a tin or sealed jar.

33
*Many wonderful memories of times shared
throughout the years
Lots of smiles and laughter to brighten up
our days
Many prayers that we prayed for each other
along the way.*

AUTHOR UNKNOWN

34
When sipping tea at the table, you don't
need to pick up your saucer with the cup.

35

The cup of tea on arrival at a country house is a thing which, as a rule, I particularly enjoy. I like the crackling logs, the shaded lights, the scent of buttered toast, the general atmosphere of leisured coziness.

P.G. WODEHOUSE,
THE CODE OF THE WOOSTERS

36

When creating a great pot of tea, use a ceramic or glass teapot. Tea brewed in a metal teapot might end up having a metallic taste.

37

Rooibos is a traditional drink containing calming tannin, healthy proteins, calcium, and trace elements.

38

The first bowl sleekly moistened throat and lips,
The second banished all my loneliness
The third expelled the dullness from my mind,
Sharpening inspiration gained
from all the books I've read.
The fourth brought forth light perspiration,
Dispersing a lifetime's troubles through my pores.
The fifth bowl cleansed ev'ry atom of my being.
The sixth has made me kin to the Immortals.
This seventh...
I can take no more.

LU TUNG

39

My copper kettle whistles merrily
And signals that it is time for tea.
The fine china cups are filled with the brew.
There's lemon and sugar and sweet cream, too.
But, best of all there's friendship, between you
and me.
As we lovingly share our afternoon tea.

MARIANNA AROLIN

40 Add your milk after you've poured the tea so you can judge how much is needed.

41
I wish we could sit down together,
And have a cup of tea,
But since we can't
When you have this one,
I hope you'll think of me.

AUTHOR UNKNOWN

42 In older times, the milk was poured into the cup first as a way to protect the surface of the china, but that isn't necessary now.

43

Rooibos grows only in the Cedarberg region near Cape Town. The plant receives its name, which means "red bush" in Afrikaans, from the green, needle-like leaves—when left out to dry, they turn a rich red color.

44

The daintiness and yet elegance of a china teacup focuses one to be gentle, to think warmly, and to feel close.

CAROL AND MALCOLM COHEN

45

Sassafras wood boiled down to a kind of tea, and tempered with an infusion of milk and sugar hath to some a delicacy beyond the China luxury.

CHARLES LAMB

46

*Thank God for tea! What would the world do
    without tea?
How did it exist? I am glad I was not born
    before tea.*

REVEREND SYDNEY SMITH

47

Besides its wonderfully sweet fruit, the
raspberry plant produces leaves that
are just right for a fruity, refreshing
infusion.

48

*I am in no way interested in immortality,
but only in the taste of tea.*

LU TUNG

49
Tea inspires friendship.

50
Ecstasy is a glass full of tea and a piece of sugar in the mouth.

ALEXANDER PUSKIN

51
My hour for tea is half-past five, and my buttered toast waits for nobody.

WILKIE COLLINES, *THE WOMAN IN WHITE*

52
Sherpa tea is usually a blend of oolong and Darjeeling teas that can be brewed at high altitudes—water boils at a lower temperature in high altitudes.

53 Hot Tea Eggnog

1 quart sweetened black tea
2 cups commercially prepared eggnog
fresh ground nutmeg to taste

In a saucepan, combine tea and eggnog.

Stir over medium heat until
the mixture is steaming.

Do not boil.

Serve immediately with a
sprinkling of ground nutmeg.

Susan Wheeler and Paul Kortepeter,
Tea with Victoria Rose

54

If you live in Korea, you might be enjoying a cup of Chrysanthemum tea—a favorite tisane, which is said to help ease headaches and fever as well as refresh the brain.

55

Cantonese speakers generally refer to their tradition as yam cha, "to drink tea," but when inviting a friend to a meal, will also mention the time of day. Throughout Guangdong Province, there are restaurants that open from five a.m. to midnight, serving morning tea, lunch tea, afternoon tea, dinner tea, and late-evening tea.

MARY ANN O'DONNELL

56

Tea began as a medicine and morphed
into a beverage of choice!

57

I take a few quick sips. "This is really good."
And I mean it. I have never tasted tea like
this. It is smooth, pungent, and instantly
addicting.

"This is from Grand Auntie," my mother
explains. "She told me 'If I buy the cheap
tea, then I am saying that my whole life
has not been worth something better.' A
few years ago she bought it for herself. One
hundred dollars a pound."

"You're kidding." I take another sip. It tastes
even better.

AMY TAN, *THE KITCHEN GOD'S WIFE*

58

Drinking a daily cup of tea will surely starve the apothecary.

CHINESE PROVERB

59

The earliest Yixing teapots date back to the beginning of the Ming Dynasty (1368–1644) in China.

60

Yixing teapots were originally made from the zisha clay of the Yixing region of China. The clay absorbs the flavors of the tea and the teapot becomes more seasoned with each use.

61

Tea inspires kindness.

62

What is the most wonderful thing for people
like myself who follow the Way of Tea? My
answer: the oneness of host and guest created
through 'meeting heart to heart' and sharing
a bowl of tea.

SOSHITSU SEN, *TEA LIFE, TEA MIND*

63

What part of confidante has that poor
teapot played ever since the kindly plant was
introduced among us. Why myriads of women
have cried over it, to be sure!...Nature meant
very kindly...when she made the tea plant; and
with a little thought, what series of pictures and
groups the fancy may conjure up and assemble
round the teapot and cup.

WILLIAM MAKEPEACE THACKERAY

64

A hearty black tea blend, Irish Breakfast is malty in flavor. The Irish drink their tea very strong, and this tea is delicious with milk and sugar.

65

Tea for two, and two for tea,
Me for you, and you for me.

IRVING CAESAR, "TEA FOR TWO"

66

Chai—a sweet, spicy black tea with honey, vanilla, fresh ginger, and spices.

67

Try a cup of ginger green tea—it's a very aromatic and spicy treat.

68

Though we eat little flesh and drink no wine,
Yet let's be merry; we'll have tea and toast;
Custards for supper, and an endless host
Of syllabubs and jellies and mince-pies,
And other such ladylike luxuries.

PERCY BYSSHE SHELLEY

69

It snowed last year too: I made a snowman and
my brother knocked it down and I knocked my
brother down and then we had tea.

DYLAN THOMAS,
A CHILD'S CHRISTMAS IN WALES

70

The first tea shipment arrived in Canada in 1716. It was imported by the Hudson Bay Company, and it took more than a year to arrive.

71

A simple tea set contains a teapot, teacup and saucer, sugar bowl, and a milk pitcher.

72

A Loving Recipe for a Perfect Cup of Tea

1—willing friend who loves to sit and share

1—grateful heart to have a friend that cares

1—beautiful garden to show us God is near

73

Tea! Thou soft, thou sober,
sage and venerable liquid…
to whose glorious insipidity,
I owe the happiest moments of my life,
let me fall prostrate.

COLLEY CIBBER

74

A formal tea service would include a teapot, teacup and saucer, sugar bowl, milk pitcher, coffeepot, hot water pot, slop bowl, and tray.

75

Read this my dears, and you will see
how to make a nice cup of tea
take teapot to kettle, not t'other way round
and when you hear that whistling sound
pour a little in the pot
just to make it nice and hot.
Pour that out and put in the tea,
loose or in bags, your choice, you see.
One bag for each two cups will do
with one extra bag to make a fine brew.
Steep 3-5 minutes then pour a cup.
Then sit right down and drink it up!

PATRICIA WINCHESTER, *AFTERNOON TEAS*

76

"Take some more tea," the March Hare said to
Alice, very earnestly.
"I've had nothing yet," Alice replied in an
offended tone, "so I can't take more."
"You mean you can't take less," said the Hatter:
"it's very easy to take more than nothing."

LEWIS CARROLL,
ALICE'S ADVENTURES IN WONDERLAND

77

Tea that grows wild is superior; garden tea takes second place.

LU YU

78

The slop bowl in formal tea sets is used to hold the discarded hot water that was used to warm the teapot. In the past, tea drinkers may have poured their remaining cold tea into the slop bowl before refilling their cup with fresh tea.

79

Rooibos tea is said to help relieve insomnia.

80

Bread and water can so easily be toast and tea.

AUTHOR UNKNOWN

81

Wouldn't it be dreadful to live in a country where they didn't have tea?

NOEL COWARD

82

Australian Lemon Myrtle tea is an all-Australian blend with a vibrant, lemony taste.

83

O' peppermint tea—
two delights per sip
as steamy hot as passion
cool as a wintry lake dip.

ASTRID ALAUDA

84

Loose-leaf tea is usually a better quality of tea than that found broken and bagged.

85

Cucumber sandwiches are a wonderful staple of tea parties. Here is a fool-proof recipe for perfect ones: slice two, peeled cucumbers into thin slices. Toss these with a dash of salt and about two tablespoons of white vinegar. Let these stand for an hour and then drain. Spread unsalted butter and a bit of cream cheese on white bread. Layer cucumbers thinly.

86

Love and scandal are the best sweeteners of tea.

HENRY FIELDING

87

When the tea leaves uncurl as hot water is poured over them, this is referred to as "the agony of the leaves."

88

What better way to suggest friendliness— and to create it—than with a cup of tea?

J. GRAYSON LUTTRELL

89

Tea is drunk to forget the din of the world.

T'IEN YIHENG

90

Tea tempers the spirits and harmonizes the mind, dispels lassitude and relieves fatigue, awakens thought and prevents drowsiness, lightens or refreshes the body, and clears the perceptive faculties.

CONFUCIUS

91

Tea was introduced to Russia in the seventeenth century when the Chinese embassy in Moscow gave a gift of tea to Czar Alexis.

92

Thousands of women, at this solemn afternoon hour, were sitting behind dainty porcelain and silver fittings, with their voices tinkling pleasantly in a cascade of solicitous little questions.

SAKI, *TEA*

93

MOCK DEVONSHIRE CREAM

A homemade version of
Devonshire cream is easy to create.

Chill a bowl and the beaters, and then whip
together ½ pint whipping cream, 1 tablespoon
sour cream, 3 tablespoons confectioners' sugar.

Keep refrigerated and enjoy with scones.

EMILIE BARNES,
THE TWELVE TEAS OF FRIENDSHIP

94

Black teas are made from leaves that are allowed to "ferment" or oxidize, then are "fired" or heated to remove most of the moisture. The heat is what turns the leaves black.

95

It is very strange, this domination of our intellect by our digestive organs. We cannot work, we cannot think, unless our stomach wills so. It dictates to us our emotions, our passions. After eggs and bacon it says, "Work!" After beefsteak and porter, it says, "Sleep!" After a cup of tea (two spoonfuls for each cup, and don't let it stand for more than three minutes), it says to the brain, "Now rise, and show your strength."

JEROME K. JEROME,
THREE MEN IN A BOAT

96

Where there's tea there's hope.

SIR ARTHUR PINERO

97

Black teas produce a hearty brew that is higher in caffeine content than other teas (but still lower than coffee).

98

Much less formal, but still traditional, is the intimate tea for a few friends. At such a get-together just tea is served to a group of five or six, who are usually gathered around the living-room coffee table. The food consists of a few delicate sandwiches or cookies; the hostess pours. This is also the perfect time for the true tea-lover to offer her guests the more exotic brands of tea.

Betty Crocker Hostess Cookbook, 1967

99

The "art of tea" is a spiritual force for us to share.

ALEXANDRA STODDARD

100

Bubble tea originated in Taiwan in the 1980s. It started as a combination of black tea, tapioca pearls, condensed milk, and honey. Bubble tea is now very popular, often served iced, and available with a variety of flavors added.

101

The grandfather plants and raises the tea bushes, the father harvests the tea, and the son drinks it.

CHINESE SAYING

102

This meal happened to be a make-believe tea, and they sat 'round the board guzzling in their greed; and really, what with their chatter and recriminations, the noise, as Wendy said, was positively deafening.

J.M. BARRIE, *PETER PAN*

103

Earl Grey tea is named after a nineteenth century British diplomat to China who enjoyed this tea blend that eventually would bear his name.

104

My experience...convinced me that tea was better than brandy, and during the last six months in Africa I took no brandy, even when sick taking tea instead.

THEODORE ROOSEVELT

105

Although my neighbors are all barbarians,
And you, you are a thousand miles away,
There are always two cups on my table.

TANG DYNASTY

106

You can never get a cup of tea large enough
or a book long enough to suit me.

C.S. LEWIS

107

Green teas are not fermented. Instead,
the leaves are steamed in large vats before
being fired.

108

Come oh come ye tea-thirsty restless ones—
the kettle boils, bubbles and sings, musically.

RABINDRANATH TAGORE

109

Green teas are delicate in flavor,
light in color, low in caffeine, and
soothing—they're usually enjoyed
without sugar, cream, or lemon.

110

Afternoon Tea should be provided, fresh
supplies, with thin bread-and-butter, fancy
pastries, cakes, etc., being brought in as other
guests arrive.

MRS. BEETON, *THE BOOK*
OF HOUSEHOLD MANAGEMENT

111

Oolong teas are produced by a relatively new process. They are partially fermented and have a taste that is stronger than green tea and more delicate than black tea.

112

Herbal teas are not actually teas but are "infusions" from the leaves, roots, seeds, or fruits of various plants such as peppermint, jasmine, or chamomile.

113

Find yourself a cup of tea,
the teapot is behind you.
Now tell me about
hundreds of things.

SAKI

114

Descending from his perch, he fell to unpacking it with great neatness and dispatch, while Rose watched him, wondering what was going to happen. Presently, out from the wrappings came a teapot, which caused her to clasp her hands with delight, for it was made in the likeness of a plump little Chinaman...Two pretty cups with covers, and a fine scarlet tray, completed the set, and made one long to have a "dish of tea," even in Chinese style, without cream or sugar.

LOUISA M. ALCOTT, *EIGHT COUSINS*

115

Herbal teas are typically decaffeinated. Some people drink infusions for various medicinal uses.

116

When creating a great pot of tea, measure a spoonful of loose tea for each cup desired. Then place the tea into a warmed and empty teapot. Heat water in a teakettle, keeping the lid on the kettle until the water boils. Pour freshly boiled water into the prepared teapot.

117

Tea inspires hospitality.

118

At last the secret is out,
as it always must come in the end,
The delicious story is ripe to tell an
*   intimate friend;*
Over tea-cups and in the square the
*   tongue has its desire;*
Still waters run deep, my dear,
There's never smoke without fire.

W.H. AUDEN

119

When creating a great pot of tea with tea bags, use one bag less than the desired number of cups.

120

Been in the sun too long? Run your bath water with several tea bags under the spout. Use oolong, green tea, or jasmine and soak your tender skin in the fragrant water.

121

Let us gather for a greeting
With our teacups filled with tea
And I'll tell you how important
Your friendship is to me.

ALDA ELLIS,
HATS OFF TO TEA

122

The Japanese tea ceremony is called *cha no yu*, which means "hot water for tea."

123

A tea strainer or infuser basket is ideal for infusing loose leaf teas. They give the leaves plenty of room to expand.

124

The cozy fire is bright and gay.
The merry kettle boils away
And hums a cheerful song.
I sing the saucer and the cup;
Pray, Mary, fill the teapot up.
And do not make it strong.

BARRY PAIN

125

In the early days when tea was very expensive, it was kept under lock and key and in the parlor where the lady of the house could keep watch of it.

126

Tea is certainly as much of a social drink as coffee, and more domestic, for the reason that the teacup hours are the family hours.

ARTHUR GRAY

127

The rooibos plant is actually a member of the legume family.

128

Rooibos is credited with many healthful properties because of its high amount of antioxidants and anti-inflammatory properties.

129

There was a teapot, in which Mma Ramotswe—the only lady private detective in Botswana—brewed tea. And three mugs—one for herself, one for her secretary, and one for the client. What else does a detective agency really need?

ALEXANDER MCCALL SMITH,
THE NO.1 LADIES' DETECTIVE AGENCY

130

The hot water is to remain upon the tea no longer than whiles you can say the Miserere Psalm very leisurely.

SIR KENELM DIGBY, *THE CLOSET OPENED*

131 TEA-LOVER'S TEA

1 part traditional tea
1 part lemon balm
3 parts fresh basil

Use one teaspoon of dried herbs
or one tablespoon of fresh herbs
to every cup of water.

Steep for several minutes.

VICTORIA MAGAZINE, FEBRUARY 1995

132

The spirit of the tea beverage is one of peace, comfort and refinement.

ARTHUR GRAY

133

Tea inspires hope.

134

If you live in Italy, you might be savoring a cup of Olive Leaf tea made from the Manzanillo and Mission olive tree leaves.

135

*I always fear that creation will expire
before teatime.*

REVEREND SYDNEY SMITH

136

Olive Leaf tea is caffeine free and said
to have properties to aid in lowering
cholesterol and blood pressure. It is
served hot or cold.

137

At your next special tea gathering, serve
your tea from a glass teapot. Add in
lavender or cinnamon sticks or edible
flowers for great visual appeal.

138

Tea to the English is really a picnic indoors.

ALICE WALKER

139

I could have introduced you to some very beautiful people. Mrs. Langtry and Lady Lonsdale and a lot of clever beings who were at tea with me.

OSCAR WILDE

140

When you keep tea away from light and moisture, the loose tea can have a shelf life of about two years.

141

Bagged tea can have a shelf life of six months.

142

What strong medicinal, but rich, scents from the decaying leaves! The rain falling on the freshly dried herbs and leaves, and filling the pools and ditches into which they have dropped thus clean and rigid, will soon convert them into tea—green, black, brown, and yellow teas, of all degrees of strength, enough to set all Nature a-gossiping.

HENRY DAVID THOREAU,
AUTUMNAL TINTS (1862)

143

Children of all ages will love jam tea. Place a teaspoon of a favorite jam in the bottom of a tea cup, pour prepared hot English Breakfast tea over the jam, and stir. If more sweetness is desired, add a bit of sugar and top with whipped cream.

144

Afternoon tea was started by Anna, seventh Duchess of Bedford, in the nineteenth century. She invited guests for tea and sweets in the afternoon to help fill the long gap between breakfast and dinner. Soon this became tradition in England and North America.

145

Tea can help keep your breath sweet!

146

Thomas Sullivan came up with the idea of sending his tea samples in a small, silk bag. He was surprised when customers started requesting the bagged tea as product! The tea bag was born.

147

Tea inspires comfort.

148

The order never varies. Two slices of bread-and-butter each, and China tea. What a hide-bound couple we must seem, clinging to custom because we did so in England. Here, on this clean balcony, white and impersonal with centuries of sun, I think of half-past four at Manderley, and the table drawn before the library fire. The door flung open, punctual to the minute, and the performance, never-varying, of the laying of the tea, the silver tray, the kettle, the snowy cloth.

DAPHNE DU MAURIER, *REBECCA*

149

Each cup of tea represents an imaginary voyage.

CATHERINE DOUZEL

150

When creating a great pot of tea, remove the kettle of water from the burner as soon as it hits a rolling boil.

151

Overboiling causes water to lose oxygen and can make your tea taste flat.

152

The music of tea is the melody that soothes me.

MORGAN CHRISTIANSEN

153

Herbal teas don't contain tea leaves but draw their flavor instead from herbs and flowers. They are called infusions or tisanes.

154

Tisanes can be made with fresh or dried flowers, leaves, seeds, or roots. Simply pour boiling water over the plant parts and let them steep for a few minutes.

155

The tea plant's official name is *Camellia sinensis*. It is a tropical evergreen with shiny, dark green leaves.

156

*The privileges of the side-table included the
small prerogatives of sitting next to the toast,
and taking two cups of tea to other people's one.*

CHARLES DICKENS

157

Traditional English Tea is served
between three and six o'clock. When
served later in the afternoon, the food
offerings are more substantial.

158

*The Baroness found it amusing to go to tea; she
dressed as if for dinner. The tea-table offered
an anomalous and picturesque repast; and on
leaving it they all sat and talked in the large
piazza, or wandered about the garden in the
starlight.*

HENRY JAMES, *THE EUROPEANS*

159

In the South a favorite beverage is sweet tea. This is tea that has sugar added either before, during, or after brewing and before the tea is cooled.

160

Nowhere is the English genius of domesticity more notably evident than in the festival of afternoon tea. The...chink of cups and the saucers tunes the mind to happy repose.

GEORGE GISSING

161

People enjoy teas from numerous countries, but most of the fine teas originate from India, Japan, China, Sri Lanka, and Formosa. Other top producers include Kenya and Turkey.

162

To protest the British taxes on tea in 1773, American women in Boston, Hartford, and other New England cities vowed to drink teas from indigenous weeds instead of imported teas. The brews they came up with were called Liberty Tea.

VICTORIA ZAK, *20,000 SECRETS OF TEA*

163

The largest source of catechins in the human diet is from various teas. Catechins have been shown to reduce the risk of cancer, lower cholesterol, and kill bacteria.

164

The longer tea brews, the more tannin is allowed to dissolve into the brew. Tannin is the compound that gives tea its pungency and body.

165

In the late 1800s green tea was frequently the tea of choice. But during World War II the sources for green tea were cut off; Americans relied on imported tea from British-controlled India, which produced black tea. After the war most tea drinkers were consuming black tea.

166

Green tea has been attributed with health benefits to help the body fight cancer, headaches, rheumatoid arthritis, high cholesterol levels, cardiovascular disease, infection, and impaired immune function.

167

White tea has strong anti-viral and anti-bacterial benefits.

168 HOT FRUITED TEA

5 cups boiling water

5 tea bags or 5 teaspoons tea

10 whole cloves

¼ teaspoon cinnamon

½ cup sugar

¼ cup lemon juice

⅓ cup orange juice

3 unpeeled orange slices, cut in half

Pour boiling water over tea, cloves, and cinnamon.
Cover and let steep 5 minutes.
Strain tea; stir in sugar and fruit juices.
Heat to just below boiling.
Serve hot with an orange slice in each cup.
6 servings.

BETTY CROCKER'S HOSTESS COOKBOOK, 1967

169

Bergamot is a citrus fruit grown in southern Italy. It is made into marmalades and liqueurs, and the oil is used in the Earl Grey blend of tea. The aromatic oil is extracted from the fruit's rind.

170

When tea first arrived in England, it was called by its Cantonese slang term—*cha*. Later the British began to call it by the local word *t'e*, or *Tay*, or *Tee*.

171

The Boston Tea Party hastened the approach of the American War of Independence.

172

Tea inspires love.

173

When enjoying your favorite tea over ice…double its strength when brewing so that it remains flavorful to the last sip.

174

"Tea for Two," a song published in 1924 with lyrics by Irving Caesar, was from the musical comedy *No No Nanette,* which opened in Detroit in April, 1924. It is one of the most familiar melodies in the world.

175

The word tea *caddy* is believed to have come either from "catty," the word for a Chinese pound or from the Malay "kati," a measure of weight about ³/₅ of a kilo.

176

While many still hold about a pound of tea, the size of tea caddies became bigger as tea became less of a luxury and more of a staple.

177

The earliest tea caddies brought to Europe from China were made of porcelain. But soon designs and materials varied greatly.

178

Orange Pekoe tea has nothing to do with oranges! It is named after the Dutch House of Orange and relates to a grading system term used to grade black teas.

179

All true tea lovers not only like their tea strong, but like it a little stronger with each year that passes.

GEORGE ORWELL,
"A NICE CUP OF TEA"

180

Black teas of the Orange Pekoe grade are fragrant with strong floral and fruity aromas. They have a slightly bitter taste but a sweet aftertaste.

181

Oolong tea is believed to help in digestion and to increase metabolism.

182

*If your tongue trips over "oolong" and there's no
     place for your spoon,
If you end up with your cookie on your knee
If dainty conversation leaves you speechless far
     too soon,
You need some help surviving Ladies' Tea.*

FROM *AFTERNOON TEA
AT PITTOCK MANSION*

183

Red tea is strong in antioxidants,
which are known to help reduce the
risk of cancer and heart problems.

184

When creating a great pot of tea, stir the
tea gently before pouring it through the
tea strainer and into the teacups.

185

The naming of teas is a difficult matter,
It isn't just one of your everyday games—
Some might think you as mad as a hatter
Should you tell them each goes by several names.
For starters each tea in this world must belong
To the families Black or Green or Oolong;
Then look more closely at these family trees—
Some include Indians along with Chinese.

T.S. ELIOT, *THE NAMING OF CATS*

186

I especially enjoy green tea in the springtime.
This bright, delicate tea has an aroma that
reminds me of dew on clover. It has a taste
that is light and soothing, so like the vernal
sunshine. And when green tea is perfumed
with jasmine, orange or rose blossoms, the
whole essence of spring seems to be dissolved
in my cup.

SUSAN WHEELER AND PAUL KORTEPETER,
TEA WITH VICTORIA ROSE

187

A regular part of Tibetan life is to drink butter tea—made from black tea leaves, yak butter, and salt.

188

Hearty teas, like blends from India and Africa, are great for morning tea.

189

Favorite blends for a morning cup of tea include Earl Grey, Taylors English Breakfast, Ceylon, Assam, Irish Breakfast, Scottish Breakfast, and South African Kwazulu.

190

For your afternoon tea pleasure, turn to teas from China. Darjeeling is a favorite.

191

Savor lighter teas in the evening. Green tea is a good choice because it has less caffeine. Or enjoy a decaffeinated tea or herbal tisane such as Chamomile.

192

When creating a great pot of tea, pour boiling water into the teapot and remember that small tea leaves will take less time to brew than large ones.

193

A cream tea is tea served alongside bread with clotted cream and jam, usually strawberry.

194

The choice of bread for a cream tea depends on the geographic location. It can be anything from a scone to a sweet bread.

195

May this tea be steeped with love
For friendships sent down from above.

SANDY LYNAM CLOUGH,
THE ART OF TEA AND FRIENDSHIP

196

To make loose-leaf tea, just measure two teaspoons of tea leaves per four-cup pot. Steep three to five minutes, then strain and serve.

197

If you live in Argentina, you'd likely be sipping Yerba Mate—a potent drink with a touch of vanilla and milk.

198

The full teapot makes no sound.

CHINESE PROVERB

199

Tea inspires renewal.

200

If you live in Egypt, you'd likely be sipping Karkade. This traditional Egyptian tea includes brewed hibiscus flowers and is served with lots of sugar.

201

If you live in the Middle East, you might be enjoying your meals with Moroccan Mint tea. This drink is sweetened with spearmint leaves.

202

There is a great deal of poetry and fine sentiment in a chest of tea.

RALPH WALDO EMERSON

203   ELIZABETH MONROE'S SHREWSBURY CAKES

¼ pound butter

1 pound brown sugar

1 egg, well beaten

12 ounces flour

———————

Mix all dry ingredients.

Add well beaten egg.

Roll, then cut with a tin mold and bake the cakes for 20 to 25 minutes in a 300 degree oven.

Note: This is a 400-year-old recipe brought to the colonies from England.

FROM THE NOVEMBER 1996
FIRST LADIES TEA PARTY MENU AND RECIPE BOOKLET,
FOUR SEASONS HOTEL, NEW YORK

204

If you live in Lebanon, you might be savoring a demitasse glass of white coffee—this tea-like drink consists of orange flowers and sugar.

205

For best results, brew green tea in water that is around 165 degrees.

206

When drinking oolong tea, the Chinese custom, to this day, is to use a tiny teapot and tiny teacup.

207

Oolong tea was first produced about 400 years ago at the end of the Ming Dynasty at Mt. Wu Yi Shan in Fujian Province.

208

Want your feet to smell fresh? Tea is a natural astringent and the tannic acid will help kill bacteria. Soak your feet in black tea for great results.

209

Genmaicha is a Japanese drink that combines tea with roasted brown rice. It was created as a way to stretch the tea during lean times. Some grains of the rice can "pop" during the roasting process so it is referred to as "popcorn tea."

210

If you live in Singapore, you might be savoring Teh Tarik (which means pull tea). It is a frothy drink made of tea and condensed milk. The froth is created by pouring the drink from high to low containers. This also cools the tea for easy drinking.

211

Ceylon tea is black tea grown in Sri Lanka, which was known as Ceylon before 1972.

212

High Tea received its name during the Victorian period when families would eat an evening meal of meats, bread, cheese, and other substantial foods along with tea. These were eaten at a high dining table.

213

When the girl returned, some hours later, she carried a tray, with a cup of fragrant tea steaming on it; and a plate piled up with very hot buttered toast, cut thick, very brown on both sides, with the butter running through the holes in it in great golden drops, like honey from the honeycomb.

KENNETH GRAHAME,
WIND IN THE WILLOWS

214

By the third century AD, tea was a daily drink in China.

215

Low Tea—the afternoon tea—was created as a time for a light snack with tea served in sitting rooms at the low tables near the sofa and chairs. Low Tea is actually the more formal tea.

216

Darjeeling tea originates from Darjeeling in West Bengal, India and is sometimes called the "Champagne of Tea."

217

England welcomed it [tea] in 1650 and spoke of it as "that excellent and by all physicians approved China drink, called by the Chineans Tcha, and by other nations Tay, alias Tee."

KAKUZO OKAKURA

218

Create a mild astringent from tea to use on your face. Pour boiling water over two tea bags of your choice and allow them to steep until cool. Remove the bags and add ¼ cup witch hazel to the cooled tea. Pour the mixture into a different container. Apply to your skin with cotton pads after cleansing.

219

She poured out Swann's tea, inquired "Lemon or cream?" and, on his answering "Cream, please," said to him with a laugh: "A cloud!" And as he pronounced it excellent, "You see, I know just how you like it." This tea had indeed seemed to Swann, just as it seemed to her; something precious, and love has such a need to find some justification for itself, some guarantee of duration, in pleasures which without it would have no existence and must cease with its passing.

MARCEL PROUST, *SWANN'S WAY*

220

A tea table is a small table used for serving afternoon tea.

221

If you're in London, head for The Dorchester for their award-winning tea. They have been presented with the prestigious *Top London Afternoon Tea Award* by The British Tea Council more times than any other London hotel.

222

His guests found it fun to watch him make tea—mixing careful spoonfuls from different caddies.

JAMES HILTON,
GOOD-BYE, MR. CHIPS

223

To best protect your teapot, hand wash it with warm water and avoid using any detergent or soap.

224

Cambric tea was hot water and milk, with only a taste of tea in it, but little girls felt grown-up when their mothers let them drink cambric tea.

LAURA INGALLS WILDER,
THE LONG WINTER

225

*Tea does our fancy aid,
Repress those vapours which the head invade
And keeps that palace of the soul serene.*

EDMUND WALLER, "OF TEA"

226

Pewter teapots were used in Colonial times by those who could not afford silver ones. Now pewter teapots are used to brew stronger teas.

227

You can infuse your meals with the taste of tea. When preparing rice or other grain dishes, substitute half of the water or broth with tea. Experiment with different combinations.

228

Steeping Tricks: For white tea, heat water until just before boiling and steep thirty seconds to two minutes.

229

Somehow, taking tea together encourages an atmosphere of intimacy when you sleep off the timepiece in your mind and cast your fate to a delight of tasty tea, tiny foods, and thoughtful conversation.

GAIL GRECO

230

Tea inspires generosity.

231

Steeping Tricks: For green tea, heat water until just before boiling and steep one to three minutes.

232

[I am a] hardened and shameless tea drinker, who has for twenty years diluted his meals only with the infusion of this fascinating plant; whose kettle has scarcely time to cool; who with tea amuses the evening, with tea solaces the midnight, and with tea welcomes the morning.

Samuel Johnson

233

Steeping Tricks: For oolong tea, heat water until just boiling and steep three to five minutes.

234

The hour...can be anywhere between three and six o'clock in the afternoon. The general rule is that the earlier tea is served, the lighter the refreshments. At three, tea is usually a snack—dainty finger sandwiches, petits fours, fresh strawberries; at six, it can be a meal—or "high" tea—with sausage rolls, salads, and trifle.

ANGELA HYNES, *THE PLEASURES OF AFTERNOON TEA*

235

Steeping Tricks: For black tea, heat water until boiling, steep three to five minutes.

236

Christopher Robin was home by this time, because it was the afternoon, and he was so glad to see them that they stayed there until very nearly tea-time, and then they had a Very Nearly tea, which is one you forget about afterwards, and hurried on to Pooh Corner, so as to see Eeyore before it was too late to have a Proper Tea with Owl.

A.A. MILNE, THE HOUSE AT POOH CORNER

237

Steeping Tricks: For herbal teas, heat water until boiling and steep for five minutes.

238

Most tea in America in revolutionary times was green tea, not black.

239 APPLE CIDER TEA

2½ teaspoons black tea leaves

2½ cups water

¼ cup sugar

juice of 2 oranges (about 1 cup)

5 cups apple cider

8 thin lemon slices

Following the traditional method, make tea from tea leaves and boiling water; allow to brew for 5 minutes. Place sugar in a large bowl or pitcher. Strain hot tea into bowl and stir until sugar is dissolved. Stir in orange juice. Just before serving, add apple cider and reheat. Pour into cups and offer slices of lemon. Serve hot or cold.

EMILIE BARNES,
THE TWELVE TEAS OF INSPIRATION

240

Steeping Tricks: Cut your tea caffeine by eighty percent by pouring a small amount of water over the tea, steep for thirty seconds, pour out that first round and refill your cup with water to steep for the full three minutes. Most of the caffeine is released from the tea in those first thirty seconds.

241

Ancient China used tea as currency. Tea leaves were compressed into a brick shape. One side of the brick was scored so that it could be divided when change was needed.

242

After you shampoo, rinse your hair with a glass of green tea mixed with some lemon juice. Leave the rinse in for silky, smooth hair.

243

In 1662 when Charles II married Catherine of Braganza, a Portuguese princess, she introduced tea to the court, and it became popular very quickly. Her dowry included the territories of Bombay and Tangier and many chests of tea.

244

Tea comes to the aid of puffy eyes. Boil water and put two black tea bags in. Brew for five minutes, remove the bags, and press out the liquid. Place the bags in the freezer for ten minutes. Lie down and place the cooled tea bags over your eyes for ten to fifteen minutes. The eye area will look refreshed. Warm tea bags can also be used.

245

In April of 1773, the British Parliament passed the Tea Act to grant the East India Company a monopoly on the American tea trade. This ignited frustrations among Americans and eventually led to the Boston Tea Party.

246

And so it continued all day, wynde after wynde, from a room beyond came the whistle of a teakettle. "Now, you really must join me. I've some marvelous Darjeeling, and some delicious petits fours a friend of mine gave me for Christmas."

MARTHA GRIMES, *THE MAN WITH A LOAD OF MISCHIEF*

247

Rosehips tea is an herbal tea high in vitamin C and antioxidants. It's made from the red fruits that form on the rosebush after the flowers fade.

248

When brewing rosehips tea using the whole rosehips, steep for ten minutes.

249

The best green tea comes from the first harvest in late April, early May.

250

In a few minutes tea was brought. Very delicate was the china, very old the plate, very thin the bread-and-butter, and very small the lumps of sugar. Sugar was evidently Mrs. Jamieson's favourite economy.

ELIZABETH GASKILL, *CRANFORD*

251

The hostess of a tea party serves the tea and makes sure that every guest has a full cup. A hostess can also ask a friend to "do the honors" of pouring tea.

252

After tea has been poured, a tea party hostess then offers milk, lemon, or sugar to her guests.

253

Ceylon tea has three categories: up-country, mid-country, and low-country. These classifications are based on the geography of the land on which it is grown.

254

Even expensive tea is a great deal. A tea that costs $100.00 per pound provides delicious cups of brewed tea that are only 50 cents each.

255

Enjoy life sip by sip not gulp by gulp.

THE MINISTER OF LEAVES

256

The type of chai most frequently enjoyed in the United States is masala chai. Masala chai includes one or more warm spices such as cardamom, cinnamon, ginger, cloves, or vanilla.

257

With each sip I taste
the fire that gives its heat.
The water that gives its wetness.
The leaf that gives its spell.
The pot that gives its emptiness.

With each lingering sip
I cannot help but see
all that makes tea
as well make me.

THE MINISTER OF LEAVES

258

Oolong leaves are commonly used
multiple times—up to three times.

259

After lunch—one short nap;
On waking up—two cups of tea.

FROM A CHINESE POEM

260

Add a tablespoon of maple syrup to your cup of tea for a sweet flavor.

261

A French tea press provides a tidy, simple way to enjoy the rich flavor of loose-leaf tea.

262

Mote spoons, which guests can use to remove any leaves that may have eluded the filter and strainer, are generally silver and have holes in the bowl. This allows the tea, but not the leaves, to drain back into the cup.

JOHN BEILENSON, *THE BOOK OF TEA*

263

Black tea, on average, has about 40 to 45 milligrams of caffeine per bag, less than half of the caffeine in a cup of coffee.

264

Green tea has about 20 milligrams of caffeine, which is a third of that in black tea.

265

Demitasse spoons are delicate, small spoons measuring about three to four inches. They are used to stir sugar, milk, or cream into cups of tea.

266

Tea poultices have been used to reduce inflammation and pain caused by skin burns.

267

Green tea tends to have stronger anti-inflammatory effects than black tea.

268

In 1890 Thomas Lipton unveiled this slogan for his successful tea company: Direct from the Tea Gardens to the Teapot.

269

Spice up your cold recovery by adding ¼ teaspoon of cayenne pepper to ½ cup of hot black tea with milk.

270

After the French Revolution and Louis XVI and Marie Antoinette lost their heads, many Frenchmen lost their appetite for tea—it represented royalty, their excesses, and their good life in contrast to the hard lives of those they taxed and ruled.

271

Use milk for your tea; cream is too heavy.

272

An Arnold Palmer drink is made with half iced tea (sweetened or unsweetened) and half lemonade. It is named after the legendary golfer.

273

Matcha is a fine, powdered green tea that is used in Japanese tea ceremonies.

274

Great as has been the influence of the tea-masters in the field of art, it is as nothing compared to that which they have exerted on the conduct of life. Not only in the usages of polite society, but also in the arrangement of all our domestic details, do we feel the presence of the tea-masters.

KAKUZO OKAKURA

275 THAI ICED TEA

¼ cup strong Thai tea
(made from Thai tea powder)

½ cup boiling water

2 teaspoons sweetened condensed milk

evaporated milk or whole milk

ice cubes

garnish with mint

Mix the Thai tea powder, boiling water, and sweetened condensed milk and stir.

Pour over ice, top off with evaporated or whole milk (do not stir in), and garnish with mint leaves.

276

The shortest distance between two strangers is a full teapot and two cups.

277

If man has no tea in him, he is incapable of understanding truth and beauty.

JAPANESE PROVERB

278

Never use lemon and milk in tea; the citrus will curdle the milk.

279

In the mid to late 1600s, the English developed the idea of tea gardens after witnessing the pleasures of Dutch tavern garden teas.

280

The English created festive, luxurious gardens where ladies and gentlemen could stroll with their tea and enjoy the entertainment of music, nature's splendor, fireworks, actor presentations, games, and more.

281

The English tea gardens provided a gathering place that included women. For the first time, women were permitted to enter a mixed, public gathering without scandal or criticism.

282

The public English tea gardens created a place where all of British society gathered, which meant a mingling of different classes and backgrounds.

283

To create oolong tea, the tea leaves are withered for a shorter period than those prepared for black tea; this produces a partially-oxidized leaf.

284

Stands the Church clock at ten to three?
And is there honey still for tea?

RUPERT BROOKE,
THE OLD VICARAGE, GRANTCHESTER

285

After picking, green tea leaves are steamed almost immediately to stop the oxidation process. They are then rolled and dried.

286

Oolong tea has about
30 milligrams of caffeine per bag.

287

New manners apply when drinking the
pu-erh tea from China—it's said to be
best when slurped. The air magnifies
the diverse flavors and allows greater
contact with your taste buds.

288

The top tea producers include China,
India, Sri Lanka, Indonesia, Turkey, and
Vietnam.

289

Production of tea in India started in the nineteenth century when Britain needed sources other than China to help quench their thirst for tea.

290

Cuppa is British informal for "a cup of tea."

291

For a special tea treat, spread a cup of sugar on a cookie sheet leaving a two-inch border. Spread butter to cover that border and then broil this combination until the sugar is caramel colored. Let it cool and then crush into small pieces to serve alongside your tea.

ALDA ELLIS, *A TABLE OF GRACE*

292

Help ease the discomfort of an insect bite or razor burn by placing a moist green tea bag over the area. The tea properties will reduce itching and swelling.

293

If you live in Mexico or South America, you might be drinking Pau d'Arco tea, which is made from the inner bark of the Pau d'Arco tree.

294

If you are cold, tea will warm you;
if you are too heated, it will cool you;
if you are depressed, it will cheer you;
if you are exhausted, it will calm you.

WILLIAM GLADSTONE

295

In the early evening of December 16, 1773, a band of men, some disguised as Mohawk American Indians, assembled on a hill near the wharf. Whooping Indian-style war cries, they marched to the wharf, where they boarded the ships one after another, hoisted the tea on board deck, split open the chests—342 in total—and threw all the tea into the sea. The whole affair took about three hours, and it was not a violent protest—the ships' crews attested that nothing had been damaged or destroyed except the tea—and the protesters swept the decks clean afterwards.

United Kingdom Tea Council, London

296

When stirring your tea, never touch the cup with your spoon. Instead, swirl the tea in the center of the cup.

297

End your day with a cup of tea for your feet! Place a few teaspoons of loose chamomile flower tea into a small tub of hot water. Add an essential oil or bath oil for aromatic pleasure. Let this steep for several minutes and then soak your feet.

298

When you want a dash more flavor or just variety, add some citrus peel, zest, or spices to your tea.

299

O Tea! O leaves torn from the sacred bough!
O stalk, gift born of the great gods!
What joyful region bored thee?
In what part of the sky
Is the fostering earth swollen with your health,
bringing increase.

PIERRE DANIEL HUET,
"TEA ELEGY" (1709)

300

As far back as 500 BC, the Chinese flavored their tea by boiling it with orange peel and spices.

301

Tea inspires joy.

302

The effect of tea is cooling and as a beverage it is most suitable. It is especially fitting for persons of self-restraint and inner worth.

LU YU (715–803), *CH'A CHING*

303

*Steam rises from a cup of tea
and we are wrapped in history,
inhaling ancient times and lands,
comfort of ages in our hands.*

FAITH GREENBOWL

304

Assam is a black tea produced in Assam, India. Blends containing Assam include English Breakfast tea, Irish Breakfast tea, and Scottish Breakfast tea.

305

In India, chai is more popular than coffee. Chai is made by boiling loose-leaf tea in a pot of milk and water.

306

*Surely every one is aware of the divine pleasures
which attend a wintry fireside; candles at
four o'clock, warm hearth rugs, tea, a fair
tea-maker, shutters closed, curtains flowing in
ample draperies to the floor, while the wind
and rain are raging audibly without.*

THOMAS DE QUINCEY

307

Tea inspires reflection.

308

Tea can be used to dye natural fabrics.
Make a new tablecloth look vintage or
give a stained curtain new life with a
sepia shade or hue from tea.

309

"Penny universities" was a term for coffeehouses in old London where men would pay a penny entrance fee and enjoy a pot of tea and engage in dialogue with peers.

310

A tea funnel is used to transfer tea leaves from the storage container into the teapot.

311

A spout needle is used to help clear trapped tea leaves from the spout of the teapot.

312 Coconut-Mint Tea
(makes 8 servings)

2 cups fresh mint leaves

8 cups double-strength, freshly brewed tea

1 cup coconut syrup

5 tablespoons fresh lemon juice

———————

Crush mint leaves with a wooden spoon.

Place mint leaves in a large teapot.

Add hot tea, coconut syrup,
and lemon juice.

If needed add more coconut syrup by
tablespoons and lemon juice by teaspoons.

EMILIE BARNES,
THE TWELVE TEAS OF INSPIRATION

313

A dregs spoon is used to remove steeped tea leaves from the teapot.

314

When friends ask for a second cup they are open to conversation.

GAIL PARENT

315

"The usual for me." The usual was a strong infusion of different kinds of Oriental teas, which raised her spirits after her siesta.

GABRIEL GARCIA MARQUEZ,
LOVE IN THE TIME OF CHOLERA

316

A tea scoop is used to pick up tea leaves from the storage container (to avoid absorbing any oils, dry tea leaves should not come into contact with one's skin).

317
Tea tongs are used to gather steeped tea leaves from the teapot.

318
Here thou, great Anna! Whom three realms obey,
Dost sometimes counsel take—and sometimes tea.

ALEXANDER POPE

319
Peter was not very well during the evening.
His mother put him to bed,
and made some chamomile tea:
"One table-spoonful to be taken at bed-
time."

BEATRIX POTTER,
THE TALE OF PETER RABBIT

320

The ancient Greeks, Romans, and Egyptians used chamomile for its medicinal properties.

321

Before the 1900s, cargo ships carrying tea usually took between 12 and 15 months to make passage from the East to London.

322

The Great Tea Race of 1866 involved clippers that carried tea. The race covered 16,000 miles, began at Foochow, China, and ended in London, England. It took 99 days.

323

Lipton Tea patented a four-sided tea bag in 1952 called the flo-thru tea bag.

324

With melted snow I boil fragrant tea.

MENICUS

325

We had a kettle; we let it leak:
Our not repairing made it worse.
We haven't had any tea for a week...
The bottom is out of the Universe.

RUDYARD KIPLING

326

Tea master Lu Yu wrote the first known book on tea, *Ch'a Ching*.

327

When serving sandwiches at a tea gathering, add variety with different types and textures of bread. Select from rye, whole wheat, raisin, date, nut, or other favorites. For color and variety use two kinds of bread in one sandwich.

328

Taza de té is Spanish for teacup.

329

SOUTHERN DEVONSHIRE CREAM

❧

1 6-ounce carton sour cream

1 8-ounce block of cream cheese

1 cup powdered sugar

_____

Cream ingredients together and beat with an
electric mixer until light and fluffy.

Place in a nice crystal bowl.

Garnish with a strawberry or snippet of mint.

ALDA ELLIS,
HATS OFF TO TEA!

330

The tea ceremony requires years of training and practice...yet the whole of this art, as to its detail, signifies no more than the making and serving of a cup of tea. The supremely important matter is that the act be performed in the most perfect, most polite, most graceful, most charming manner possible.

LAFCADIO HEARN

331

Porcelain manufacturers in Europe and Russia first revealed a taste and flair for rose-patterned pieces during the seventeenth and eighteenth centuries.

332

Tea inspires beauty.

333

Infuse your cup of tea with more fragrance and flavor. When lavender is in bloom, float a fresh blossom in your cup. It is most refreshing.

334

There are few hours in life more agreeable than the hour dedicated to the ceremony known as afternoon tea.

HENRY JAMES, *PORTRAIT OF A LADY*

335

Cynthia came in quietly and set a cup of tea before him. He kissed her hand, inexpressibly grateful, and she went back into the kitchen. When we view the little things with thanksgiving, even they become big things.

JAN KARON, *THESE HIGH, GREEN HILLS*

336

Tea's proper use is to amuse the idle, and relax the studious, and dilute the full meals of those who cannot use exercise, and will not use abstinence.

SAMUEL JOHNSON

337

The typical kind of crumpet served with tea is a Scottish crumpet, which is browned on one side and lightly cooked on the other, porous side.

338

Tea is wealth itself,
Because there is nothing that cannot be lost,
No problem that will not disappear,
No burden that will not float away,
Between the first sip and the last.

THE MINISTER OF LEAVES

339

Tea inspires community.

340

Tea at the Ritz is the last delicious morsel of
Edwardian London. The light is kind, the
cakes are frivolous and the tempo is calm,
confident and leisurely.

HELEN SIMPSON, *THE LONDON RITZ
BOOK OF AFTERNOON TEA*

341

A combination of fine tea, enchanting objects
and soothing surroundings exerts a therapeutic
effect by washing away the corrosive strains
and stress of modern life…[it] induces a mood
that is spiritually refreshing…[and produces] a
genial state of mind.

JOHN BLOFELD

342

Tasse de thé is French for teacup.

343

I'm sending you love and tea,
To warm your winter's day.
Think of me as you pour your cup
And all the good things we would say.
If we could be together now
Instead of miles apart,
We'd sip our teas and memories,
The sweet warmth fills the heart.

SUSAN YOUNG

344

Tea inspires gratitude.

345

*Those dripping crumpets, I can see them now.
Tiny crisp wedges of toast, and piping-hot,
flaky scones. Sandwiches of unknown nature,
mysteriously flavoured and quite delectable,
and that very special gingerbread. Angel cake,
that melted in the mouth, and his rather
stodgier companion, bursting with peel and
raisins. There was enough food there to keep a
starving family for a week.*

DAPHNE DU MAURIER, *REBECCA*

346

*The tea party is a spa for the soul. You leave
your cares and work behind. Busy people
forget their business. Your stress melts away,
your senses awaken.*

ALEXANDRA STODDARD

347  LAVENDER HONEY

2 cups pale honey
several pieces of lavender

In a saucepan, stir the honey
over medium heat.

Place the lavender in a jelly jar and then pour
the warmed honey over the lavender.

Cool and then cover with a tight lid.

Serve after a day or two to allow
the honey to set.

This is great on scones, biscuits, or drizzled
into your next cup of tea.

348

When world-class alpinists summit the highest mountains on earth, they become so exhausted and cold that their bodies can't digest most food. Only by melting snow and making tea are they able to keep functioning.

GENE SKINNER

349

The ritual of tea is the perfect complement for your time of prayer and meditation.

350

It is safe to say that when the water boils, as it surely will, given enough heat under it, it is ready. Then, at that moment and no other, pour it into the teapot.

M.F.K. FISHER

351

When the tea is brought at five o'clock
And all the neat curtains are drawn with care,
The little black cat with bright green eyes
Is suddenly purring there.

HAROLD MONROE (1879–1932),
"MILK FOR THE CAT"

352

You can serve high tea around the dining
room table, but afternoon tea is more of
a living room occasion, with everything
brought in on a tray or a cart.

ANGELA HYNES, *THE PLEASURES
OF AFTERNOON TEA*

353

Sherpa tea is frequently used to raise the internal body temperature and prevent hypothermia in mountain hikers. It's common practice to make it in the same pot that the last meal was cooked in and before the pot is cleaned. This salvages food from the pot and adds flavor and nutrients to the tea.

354

Bedouin tea is a green, processed tea from West Africa. It is strong, bitter, brewed double-strength (thick), and drunk through a sugar rock or cube held between the front teeth.

WWW.THETEASHOP.COM

355

[Tea-masters] have given emphasis to our natural love of simplicity, and shown us the beauty of humility. In fact, through their teachings tea has entered the life of the people.

KAKUZO OKAKURA

356

"I can just imagine myself sitting down at the head of the table and pouring out the tea," said Anne, shutting her eyes ecstatically. *"And asking Diana if she takes sugar! I know she doesn't but of course I'll ask her just as if I didn't know."*

LUCY MAUD MONTGOMERY,
ANNE OF GREEN GABLES

357

Thai iced tea with milk is called cha yen. Tea without milk is called cha dum yen.

358

There is no trouble so great or grave that cannot be much diminished by a nice cup of tea.

BERNARD-PAUL HEROUX

359

Tea...is a religion of the art of life.

KAKUZO OKAKURA

360

The morning cup of coffee has an exhilaration about it which the cheering influence of the afternoon or evening cup of tea cannot be expected to reproduce.

OLIVER WENDELL HOLMES, SR.

361

You are going out for tea today,
So mind how you behave;
Let all accounts I hear of you
Be pleasant ones, I crave.

KATE GREENAWAY

362

Tea inspires celebration.

363

One sip of this will bathe the drooping spirits in
delight, beyond the bliss of dreams.

MILTON

364

Tea inspires wholeness.

365

There is the size of the leaf:
Its unique shape,
Its unique color,
Its unique fragrance,
A taste all its own,
And it changes...sip by sip.

RON RUBIN, *TEA CHINGS*

BIBLIOGRAPHY

The following websites were
helpful sources of information:

---

www.bigelowtea.com

www.serendipitea.com

www.stashtea.com

www.tea.co.uk

THE TWELVE TEAS® OF INSPIRATION
Emilie Barnes, Paintings by Susan Rios

Participating in teatime is an act of connection, community, and pure inspiration. Bestselling author Emilie Barnes illuminates 12 themed teas that honor milestones, special people, and everyday moments—

- Words to Live By
- New Beginning
- Role Model
- Thankful Heart
- A Thing of Beauty

Artist Susan Rios' paintings transport readers to the place of possibility alongside each tea's fresh ideas and delicious recipes. The party-giver needs only to add the fellowship of great friends, family, and neighbors and her own personal touch.

To learn more about books by Harvest House Publishers
or to read sample chapters, log on to our website:

www.harvesthousepublishers.com

HARVEST HOUSE PUBLISHERS

EUGENE, OREGON